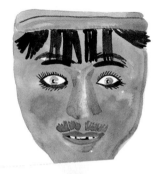

THE
FESTIVE FOOD
OF
MEXICO

Elisabeth Lambert Ortiz

ILLUSTRATED BY SALLY MALTBY

KYLE CATHIE LIMITED

In memory
my late husband, César Ortiz-Tinoco

First published 1992 by
Kyle Cathie Limited
3 Vincent Square London SW1P 2LX

Copyright © 1992 by Elisabeth Lambert Ortiz
Illustrations copyright © 1992 by Sally Maltby

ISBN 1 85626 060 7

A CIP catalogue record for this book is available from
the British Library

Designed by Geoff Hayes

Contents

La Noche Vieja

NEW YEAR'S EVE

There are no special dishes for New Year's Eve though it is celebrated with enthusiasm. There are private parties and as well many people go to restaurants where they have their favourite dishes and stay up much later than usual, in fact until the Old Year dies and the New Year is born. In addition to lavish food there will be a great variety of drinks, including tequila, wine and Mexico's excellent beers. Toasts to the New Year and wishes of Feliz *Año Nuevo*, happy New Year, to friends and relations are made in champagne or a special favourite, sparkling cider, until finally the revellers get to bed, tired but happy.

The following day sees *Menudo Estilo Sonora* come into its own as a lifesaver after a too late, over-indulgent night. Served for breakfast whenever that may be, it is wonderfully restorative. Like a *pot-au-feu*, it is both soup and meat.  When served to help the hangover sufferer, traditional wisdom advises a generous helping of the crumbled *chile péquin*, small hot dried red chiles, served with the dish. If hominy, large white corn kernels, are not available, frozen corn kernels are the best substitute.

Menudo Estilo Sonora
(TRIPE SOUP SONORA-STYLE)

serves 6

900g/2lb honeycomb tripe
2 pig's feet, halved
1 bunch spring onions, trimmed and chopped, using
    some of the green part
450g/1lb canned hominy, or frozen whole corn
    kernels
50g/2oz/1cup chopped fresh coriander leaves
salt, freshly ground black pepper
fresh oregano, chopped, or dried oregano, crumbled
dried *péquin chiles,* (dried red) crumbled
1 large (Bermuda or Spanish) onion, finely chopped
6 lime or lemon wedges

1 Put the tripe and pig's feet into a large saucepan
with salted water to cover. Bring to a simmer and
cook, covered, over low heat until the meats are
tender, about 3 hours. Check the tripe from time to
time and remove it as soon as it is tender. Tripe is
precooked and exact cooking time is difficult to
assess.
2 Cool the meats in the stock. Lift out the tripe and
cut it into squares or strips. Remove the bones from
the pig's feet and cut into pieces. Return the meats to
the stock.
3 Add the spring onions, corn, coriander and salt and
pepper to taste. Simmer over low heat for 5 minutes.
4 Serve in deep soup bowls, with small bowls of
oregano, chiles and onions, and the lime or lemon
wedges on the side, add to the soup according to
taste.

Día de los Reyes

KING'S DAY

This is 6th January, Twelfth Night, Epiphany, the day when the Three Kings came to visit Jesus with their gifts and is the traditional day in Mexico for children to receive their Christmas gifts. Having found out about Santa Claus many of them expect presents on Christmas Day as well but they can be sure of getting a gift on King's Day. This is the day when the *Rosca de Reyes* is baked. This is a ring-shaped yeast bread decorated with candied fruits and sugar and with a tiny china doll, representing the infant Jesus, baked in it. Whoever gets the china doll must give a party on 2nd February, Candlemas Day, the day of godparents.

Rosca de Reyes

(KING'S DAY RING)

3 teaspoons active dry yeast
5ml/1teaspoon sugar
50ml/2fl oz/¼cup lukewarm water
275g/10oz/2½cups plain flour
½teaspoon salt
50g/2oz/¼cup sugar
2 large eggs, well beaten
4 large egg yolks
100g/4oz/½cup butter, softened
grated rind of 1 lemon
225g/8oz/1½cups mixed chopped candied fruits and
    peels
1 small china doll
100g/4oz/1cup icing (confectioner's) sugar
40ml/2tablespoons cream
maraschino cherries, halved

1 In a small bowl proof the yeast with the sugar and water for 15 minutes or until foamy.

2 In a large bowl mix half the flour with the salt, sugar, eggs, egg yolks, butter, grated lemon rind, yeast and water and beat until the mixture is well blended.

3 Dust two-thirds of the candied fruits and peels with flour and add to the mixture. Add the remaining flour and mix to a soft dough. If it is sticky, add a little more flour. Turn onto a lightly floured board and knead until it is smooth and satiny, about 5 minutes. Shape into a ring, tucking the china doll into the dough.

4 Place on a greased baking sheet, put an egg cup or 10cm/4in jar in the centre of the ring to keep it open, cover with a cloth and leave in a warm, draft-free place to double in bulk, about 2 hours. Brush the ring with melted butter and bake in a preheated180°C/ 350°F/gas4 oven for 30 minutes, cool and transfer to a flat serving platter. Mix the icing sugar with the cream and spread over the ring. Decorate with the remaining fruits and candied peel and the halved maraschino cherries.

Tamalada

Any excuse will serve for a festive *tamalada* – a birthday, an engagement, a family reunion – the only essential being to have someone who makes really splendid *tamales*. My husband's grandmother was famous for her *tamaladas*, and would co-opt neighbours to help in the three-day cooking effort. The party would be held in her garden, which was a large one, with tables and chairs set out for guests, long tables loaded with plates of *tamales*, salads, fruit and sweetmeats, jugs of soft drinks, bottles of tequila with bowls of quartered limes, beer and wine. Perhaps there would be music, as well as lively talk and a great consumption of *tamales* with many different fillings. As soon as one platter was finished, another would arrive from the kitchen to disappear with equal speed. 'Blind' *tamales*, that is unstuffed ones, are often eaten as bread and in some households where a very light supper, *merienda*, is the evening meal, they may be eaten with either of the corn drinks, *atole* or *champurrado*. They sometimes accompany *Mole Poblano* but more often leftover *mole* is used as a filling. For dessert there are sweet *tamales* and Emperor Moctezuma's favourite stuffing for sweet *tamales* was fresh strawberries sweetened with honey.

Tamales

makes 12

12–24 dried cornhusks
75g/3oz/⅓cup lard, softened
275g/10oz/2cups *masa harina* (flour for corn tortillas)
7ml/1½teaspoons baking powder
7ml/1½teaspoons salt
350ml/12fl oz/1½cups warm chicken stock

12

1 If the cornhusks are very small, double them up. If cornhusks are not available use 20cm x 10cm/8in x 4in sheets of aluminium foil topped with pieces of greaseproof paper or kitchen parchment. Soak the cornhusks in hot water until softened.

2 In a bowl cream the lard until it is very light and fluffy. Mix the *masa harina* with the baking powder and salt and beat in the lard bit by bit. Gradually beat in the stock, a little at a time, to make a mushy dough. To test whether the dough is ready drop a little into a glass of cold water. It should float. If it sinks to the bottom and disintegrates it needs more beating. Continue to beat until the dough is light enough to float.

3 shake excess water from the cornhusks. Spread 1 tablespoon of the dough on the centre of each husk, leaving enough room to fold over the ends at top and bottom. Place 1 tablespoon of filling at the centre of the dough. Fold the cornhusk over so that the filling is completely covered by the dough. Fold the ends of the husks over at top and bottom and place, bottom ends down, in a steamer, and steam for about 1 hour, or until the dough comes away from the husks. If using foil and greaseproof or parchment paper, twist the ends to make the package watertight. Eat the *tamales* hot.

for the fillings:

Tamales may be filled with a variety of fish, poultry or meats and different sauces. Leftover *Mole Poblano* made with either turkey or chicken is a popular filling. Sometimes there is leftover *mole* sauce and this can be used with cooked, shredded pork or any poultry. *Enchilada* Sauce (page 21) can be used if the cream is left out. The filling for *Empanadas de Vigilia* (page 25) makes a good one for *tamales*, so does *Picadillo* (Minced Beef, see page 14) with a little tomato sauce.

13

Picadillo
(MINCED BEEF)

serves 6 as main course if the quantities are doubled
40ml/2tablespoons olive oil
450g/1lb lean beef mince
1 onion, finely chopped
1 garlic clove, chopped
1 tart apple, peeled, cored and chopped
225g/½lb tomatoes, peeled and chopped
2 fresh hot green chiles, seeded and chopped
40g/1½oz seedless raisins
12 pimiento-stuffed olives, halved
⅛teaspoon thyme
⅛teaspoon oregano
salt, freshly ground black pepper
25g/1oz flaked almonds

1 Heat the oil in a heavy frying-pan and brown the
beef over moderate heat. Add the onion and garlic
and cook until the onion is browned. Add the apple,
tomatoes, chiles, raisins, olives, thyme, oregano and
salt and pepper, stir to mix and cook, uncovered, until
done, about 20 minutes.
2 Fry the almonds in a little olive oil until they are
golden, and sprinkle on top of the *picadillo*. Cook for
a few minutes longer if there is much liquid. The hash
should be quite dry.

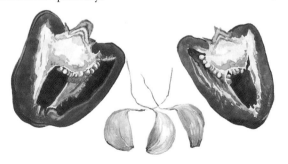

Salsa de Adobo
(ADOBO SAUCE)

In Spain *adobo* is a pickle sauce. In Mexico it is a thick chile marinade which usually contains a little vinegar. If Mexican *guajillo* chiles are unobtainable, substitute crumbled dried chiles.

makes about 225ml/8fl oz/1cup
6 dried *ancho* peppers, or use 6 fresh red peppers
6 garlic cloves
¼teaspoon ground black pepper
1 dried bay leaf, crumbled
pinch of ground cumin
½teaspoon dried oregano
½teaspoon dried thyme
40ml/2tablespoons guajillo chiles or crumbled dried chiles
50ml/2fl oz/¼cup cider vinegar

1 If using dried *ancho* peppers remove the stems, shake out the seeds, tear up roughly and soak in warm water for 20 minutes. Drain and purée in a food processor or blender with the garlic.
2 If using fresh peppers, remove the stems and seeds, chop and reduce to a purée with the garlic cloves. Add the pepper, bay leaf, cumin, oregano, and thyme, a little of the soaking water from the dried peppers, and the chiles and reduce to a thick purée.
3 If using the sauce for main courses, stir in the vinegar and pour into a glass jar. It will keep, refrigerated, for several weeks. If using it as a sauce with *tamales*, heat 2 tablespoons vegetable oil in a frying-pan and sauté the mixture, stirring constantly, over moderate heat for 5 minutes. Cool. Stuff the *tamales* with 1 tablespoon shredded chicken, pork or fish or whatever is being used, then top with 2 teaspoons of the *adobo* sauce. Steam the *tamales* in the usual way.

Tamal de Oaxaca
(OAXACAN-STYLE TAMALES)

Instead of cornhusks, banana leaves are used for these *tamales*. The banana leaves are softened in boiling water and trimmed into squares. The *tamales* are flat and square and have a subtle but distinct flavour from the leaves. A special chile from the region, *chile chilhuacle*, is used to make *Mole Negro* which like *Mole Poblano* contains a little unsweetened chocolate and is the special *mole* dish of this semi-tropical region.

Salsa de Tomate Verde
(GREEN TOMATO SAUCE)

The green tomatoes in this sauce are not ordinary, unripe tomatoes. They are the fruits *of Physalis ixocarpa* and have a number of names including husk tomato which refers to their loose brown papery outer covering. The Aztecs called them *miltomatl*; they are also called *tomatitto* and less frequently *fresadilla*. Probably the most used name is *tomatillo* (little tomato). They have a unique flavour which characterized the cooking of the Aztec and Maya empires. They are available tinned and are increasingly available fresh. If used fresh they should not be peeled as nothing would be left of them but tiny seeds! They make a wonderful sauce for *tamales* and *enchiladas*; in fact they go with any Mexican dish. Taste the liquid in the tin before adding it to the sauce as it may be salty.

2x450g/1lb tins Mexican green tomatoes
1 medium onion, finely chopped
1 garlic clove, chopped
1-2 fresh hot green chiles, seeded and chopped
120ml/6tablespoons fresh coriander leaves, chopped
40ml/2tablespoons vegetable oil   salt

16

1 In a food processor or blender combine all the ingredients except the oil and reduce to a purée. Add a little of the liquid from the tinned tomatoes if necessary. Heat the oil in a frying-pan, add the purée and cook, stirring, over moderate heat until it is slightly thickened. Season to taste with salt. Use with any savoury *tamal*.

Tamales de Dulce
(SWEET TAMALES)

1 Make a recipe for plain *tamales* (pages 12–13) but reduce the salt to 2.5ml/½teaspoon. (Use the chicken stock even though the *tamales* are sweet – between 125g/4oz/½cup and 225g/8oz/1cup granulated sugar to the *masa harina* according to taste.

2 Prepare the cornhusks and spread with a layer of dough. Top with a tablespoon of combined seedless raisins, slivered almonds and chopped citron for each *tamal*. Roll up and steam. Eat hot.Instead of almonds, pine nuts can be used and the *tamales* can also be filled with a mixture of chopped candied fruits such as pineapple, apricots, cherries or peaches. Some cooks like to colour the sweet *tamal* light pink in which case mix 1½ tablespoons grenadine syrup into the *masa* (dough).

Fiesta de la Candelaria

CANDLEMAS DAY

February 2nd is the day when whoever has found the doll figurine in the King's Day Ring must reciprocate with a party. It is also known as the day of the *padrinos*, godparents' day, and marks the real end of the Christmas festivities. The foods served are *tamales* stuffed with pork in a green chile sauce and a special, very old Mexican drink, *Champurrado*, Chocolate *Atole*. Father Sahagún, a Spanish priest in Mexico at the time of the Conquest, mentions women being given *atole*, a corn gruel, at a banquet of Aztec merchants when the men were drinking chocolate, a drink forbidden to women. *Champurrado* is a colonial drink, a compromise as women were allowed it despite the fact that it was based on chocolate. *Masa harina*, the special corn (maize) meal that is used to make *tortillas*, is the thickening agent.

Champurrado
(CHOCOLATE *ATOLE*)

serves 4–6
100g/4oz/1cup *masa harina* (*tortilla* flour)
700ml/1¼pints/3cups water
small piece cinnamon stick or 1 vanilla bean
225g/8oz/1cup light brown sugar
700ml/1¼pints/3cups milk
75g/3oz unsweetened chocolate, grated

1 Combine the *masa harina* and water in a saucepan and stir to mix. Add the cinnamon stick or vanilla

bean and cook over low heat, stirring constantly, until the liquid has thickened.

2 Remove from the heat and add the sugar, milk and chocolate stirring to mix. Discard the cinnamon stick and vanilla. Return the mixture to the heat and bring to a simmer. Serve hot in small cups or mugs.

To make *Tamales de Puerco en Salsa de Tomate Verde* (Pork Tamales in Green Tomato Sauce) have ready pork loin cooked and shredded. Combine it with *Salsa de Tomate Verde* (Green Tomato Sauce) (*Tamalada*, page 12) and use as a filling for *tamales*.

Viernes de Dolores

FRIDAY OF THE SEVEN SORROWS

During Lent, on the Friday before Good Friday, there is a fiesta the origins of which go back a long way. Called Friday of Sorrow or Friday of the Virgin of the Seven Sorrows, it was once a favourite fiesta of artists and writers who came early in the morning to eat *tamales* and drink *atole* for breakfast. It was also a *charro* festival with traditionally dressed horsemen, who came accompanied by girls dressed as the China *Poblana*, also on horseback; all immensely colourful. More recently the festival has been at the floating gardens of Xochimilco just outside Mexico City. The ancient city of Tenochtitlán was built on a lake with canals and artificial islands. Xochimilco is all that survives. Called the Venice of Mexico, it is extremely popular and somehow this sad day has become identified with a brilliant and happy fiesta where there are prizes for the best decorated boat taking people through the canals, for the best typical dancers, the best typical costume, the best singer, best guitar player and so on. Everything is decked with flowers, especially carnations and the festival ends at the village of Santa Anita, where the revellers will eat a breakfast of *enchiladas* or hot *tamales* with *atole* or *champurrado*. Sorrow seems to have been forgotten.

20

Enchiladas Rojas con Queso
(TORTILLAS STUFFED WITH CHEESE)

serves 4

First make a *Salsa Para las Enchiladas, Enchilada*
    Sauce, as follows:
1 onion, finely chopped
1 garlic clove, chopped
2 fresh hot green chiles, or more to taste, seeded and
    chopped
700g/1½lb tomatoes, peeled and chopped
salt
pinch sugar
40ml/2tablespoons vegetable oil
225ml/8fl oz/1cup soured or heavy cream

1 In a food processor or blender, combine the onion,
garlic, chiles, tomatoes, salt and sugar and reduce to a
purée.
2 In a large frying-pan heat the oil and pour in the
puree. Cook, stirring, over moderate heat until the
sauce is thick and well blended, about 5 minutes.
Cool the sauce slightly then stir in the cream. Set
aside.

To assemble the dish, have ready:
12 *tortillas*
225g/8oz/2cups grated Cheshire or mild Cheddar
    cheese (Mexicans will use *Queso de Chichuahua*)
1 onion, finely chopped
oil for frying

21

1 In a large frying-pan heat the oil and fry the *tortillas*, one by one, for about 30 seconds on each side. Drain on kitchen towels. Warm the sauce but do not let it boil as it will curdle. Dip the *tortillas* one by one in the sauce then fill with cheese and top with onion. Leave enough cheese and onion for the garnish.

2 Roll up the *tortillas* and put them into an ovenproof dish. Pour the remaining sauce over the *tortillas*, sprinkle with the remaining cheese and onion and put the dish into a preheated 180°C/350°F/gas4 oven for about 10 minutes to heat through. Serve as soon as possible as *enchiladas* go soggy if left to stand.

These *enchiladas* can be served on fast days. Another suitable stuffing would be scrambled eggs, about 6 for 12 *tortillas*. On non-fast days, favourite fillings are shredded cooked chicken breasts or shredded cooked pork.

Instead of tomato sauce, leftover sauce from *Mole Poblano* can be used.

OSARIO

FAMILIA PUCH.

Atole de Leche
(MILK ATOLE)

Father Sahagún recorded a great deal of information about the Aztec cuisine including the *atoles* or corn drinks. This is an early colonial version of the drink since the Aztecs had no cattle and therefore no milk. It remains popular throughout Mexico today. The corn (maize) flour, *masa harina* used to make *tortillas*, is the thickening agent.

serves 4–6
50g/2oz/½cup *masa harina*
700ml/1¼pints/3cups water
4cm/1½in piece cinnamon stick,
    or 1 vanilla bean
225g/8oz/1cup sugar
700ml/1¼pints/3cups milk

1 Combine the *masa harina* with the water in a large saucepan, mixing thoroughly. Add the cinnamon stick or vanilla bean and cook over low heat, stirring well, until the mixture is smooth and thick. Draw off the heat, and add the sugar and milk.
2 Return to the heat and cook at a simmer, stirring, until the sugar has dissolved.
3 Discard the cinnamon stick or vanilla bean and serve hot in cups.

Temporada de Cuaresma

LENT

During the forty days of Lent there are a number of dishes traditionally eaten on the fast days, including them *Caldo de Habas*. Fresh lima beans make a good substitute.

Caldo de Habas
(FRESH broad BEAN SOUP)

serves 6

450g/1lb broad beans, or lima beans
1 medium onion, chopped
2 garlic cloves, chopped
2litres/3½pints/6cups vegetable stock
50g/2oz lard or 4tablespoons vegetable oil
350g/12oz tomatoes, peeled and chopped
1tablespoon each chopped mint and fresh coriander
  leaves, chopped
225g/8oz tin cactus paddles (*nopalitos*) rinsed and
  chopped (optional)
salt, freshly ground black pepper

1 In a large saucepan combine the beans, onion, garlic and vegetable stock and simmer, covered, until the vegetables are very soft. Remove the solids from the soup and purée them in a food processor or blender. Return them to the liquid.
2 In a frying-pan heat the lard or vegetable oil, add the tomatoes and cook over moderate heat until they are well blended and thick. Add to the soup with the herbs and the cactus paddles, if available. Season with salt and pepper to taste. Simmer for 2–3 minutes and serve hot in soup bowls.

Empanadas de Vigilia
(LENTEN TURNOVERS)

Popular in the Lenten period of abstinence from meat are *empanadas* with a special filling. Though fasting is no longer strictly observed these good dishes survive in the traditional kitchen.

serves 8
for the pastry:
225g/8oz/2cups plain flour
1teaspoon baking powder
½teaspoon salt
175g/6oz lard, or half lard/half butter cut into bits
cold water

1 Sift the flour, baking powder and salt into a large bowl. Using the fingertips rub the fat into the flour until it resembles a coarse meal. Make a fairly stiff dough with a little cold water, gather the dough into a bowl and refrigerate, covered with greaseproof paper, for 1 hour.
2 Roll out onto a lightly floured surface to 3mm/⅛in thick and cut into 8 15cm/6in circles. Set aside.

for the filling:
80ml/4tablespoons vegetable oil
350g/12oz bass
225g/½lb tomatoes, peeled and chopped
1 medium onion, chopped
12 pimiento-stuffed olives, halved
2tablespoons capers
salt, freshly ground black pepper
1 small egg beaten with ½teaspoon water

1 Heat half the oil in a frying-pan and sauté the fish gently for about 5 minutes on each side, or until the flesh is opaque. Cool and remove all skin and bones.

Flake the fish and set aside.

2 In a food processor or blender purée the tomatoes and onion. Heat the remaining oil in a frying-pan and cook the tomato mixture until it is well blended and most of the moisture evaporated, about 10 minutes. Add the olives, capers and fish and season with salt and pepper. Spoon about 2 tablespoons of the filling across the centre of each circle of pastry, stopping short of the edges. Moisten the edges of the pastry with the egg and fold over to make a turnover, pressing the edges firmly together. Prick the tops in 2 or 3 places with the tines of a fork and brush with the egg. Bake on an ungreased baking sheet in a preheated 200°C/400°F/gas6 oven and bake for 10 minutes, then reduce the heat to 180°C/350°F/gas4 and bake for 30 minutes longer, or until golden brown. Serve as a first course.

Capirotada
(BREAD PUDDING)

This very special bread pudding is a great favourite during Lent and for any vigil before a feast day in Mexico. This recipe was given to me by my husband's grandmother, Doña Carmen Sarabia de Tinoco, who was a gifted cook.

serves 6–8
for the syrup:
450g/1lb brown sugar, firmly packed
5cm/2in piece stick cinnamon
1 small white onion stuck with 2 cloves
1 medium green pepper, seeded and sliced
peel from 1 medium orange, thinly sliced
25g/1oz/½cup fresh coriander leaves, chopped
1 medium tomato, peeled, seeded and chopped
1litre/1¾pints/4cups water

1 Combine all the ingredients in a large saucepan, bring to a simmer and cook, partially covered over low heat for 30 minutes. Cool, strain and discard the solids. Set the syrup aside.

for the pudding:
8 slices freshly toasted firm white bread cut into
    1.2cm/½in cubes
3 tart cooking apples, peeled, cored and thinly sliced
150g/5oz/1cup seedless raisins
100g/4oz/1cup chopped blanched almonds
225g/8oz Cheddar or Monterey Jack, chopped

1 Butter a 2litre/3½pint ovenproof casserole or soufflé dish and make a layer of toast cubes. Pile on layers of apples, raisins, almonds and cheese until all the ingredients are used up. Pour over the syrup and bake in a preheated 180°C/350°F/gas4 oven for 45 minutes or until heated through. Serve hot.

Arroz a la Mexicana

(RICE, MEXICAN-STYLE)

This is Mexico's most popular *sopa seca*, dry soup, that comes as a separate course after soup and before the main course at *comida*, the principal meal of the day, eaten at about 2pm or later. It is hard to imagine a festive meal without it and it is equally suitable for vigils and feasts.

serves 6–8
450g/1lb long grain rice
225g/8oz tomatoes, peeled, seeded and chopped
1 medium onion, chopped
2 garlic cloves, chopped
60ml/3tablespoons vegetable oil
800ml/1½pints/3½cups chicken stock
2 carrots, scraped and thinly sliced
175g/6oz/1cup fresh raw peas or frozen peas, thawed
1 fresh hot green chile, seeded and chopped or more
   to taste
20ml/1tablespoon fresh chopped coriander leaves or
   flat parsley

1 Wash the rice well in several changes of water and let it soak for 20 minutes. Drain thoroughly in a sieve.
2 In a blender or food processor reduce the tomatoes, onion and garlic to a purée. Heat the oil in a casserole and sauté the rice over low heat stirring constantly until it is pale gold. Do not let it brown. Add the tomato mixture and cook, stirring from time to time until the moisture has evaporated. Stir in the chicken stock, carrots, peas and chile.
3 Bring to a simmer, cover and cook over very low heat until the rice is tender and the stock absorbed, about 20 minutes. Serve garnished with the coriander or parsley.

Sábado de Gloria

EASTER SATURDAY

This is the 'little resurrection' celebrated with firecrackers because Christ has risen. It is the day when Judas gets his comeuppance from the people of Mexico. Everywhere there are cardboard figures of Judas with horns and a tail, some of them gigantic, all with firecrackers attached which burn the cardboard figures when the firecrackers are lit. The 'big resurrection' is on Sunday when Christ is in Heaven completely restored and in glory, and the church is no longer in mourning with the statues of saints and the apostles covered. A favourite dish is *Revoltijo*, a vegetable *fricasée* made with a local green vegetable *romeritos*, which looks like rosemary but has thin

fleshy leaves. These have to be stripped off the woody stems before the vegetable can be cooked. Any leafy green vegetable can be used. Spinach is a good substitute. *Revoltijo* is accompanied by shrimp fritters. At this time of year there is bound to have been a dish of *Mole Poblano* (see page 43.) Traditionally the sauce accompanying the turkey is abundant and some could easily be put aside and refrigerated for other dishes, such as *Revoltijo* (see opposite).

Revoltijo
(VEGETABLE FRICASÉE)

serves 4–6

450g/1lb *romeritos*, or any greens such as spinach,
  cooked and chopped
1 x 275g/10oz tin *nopalitos* (cactus paddles) rinsed
  and drained, or substitute 225g/8oz French beans,
  cooked and coarsely chopped
6 small new potatoes, cooked, peeled and quartered
225g/8oz/1cup dried shrimps
60ml/3tablespoons freshly made breadcrumbs
2 large eggs, lightly beaten
salt
vegetable oil
450ml/16fl oz/2cups *Mole Poblano* sauce

1 On a platter assemble all the cooked ingredients. In
a saucepan combine half the dried shrimps with
enough water to cover, bring to a simmer and cook,
uncovered for 20 minutes. Drain and set aside with
the cooked ingredients.
2 Clean the remaining dried shrimps and grind them
in a food processor or blender. In a bowl combine the
ground shrimps with the breadcrumbs and the eggs
adding more breadcrumbs if necessary to give the
mixture sufficient body. Season with salt, if necessary.
3 In a frying-pan heat the oil, enough to reach a
depth of about 2.5cm/1in, and fry the shrimp mixture
1 tablespoon at a time until lightly browned on both
sides. Drain on paper towels and keep warm.
4 In a casserole or saucepan heat the *mole* sauce, add
the *romeritos* or other greens, cactus pieces or French
beans, potatoes and boiled shrimps. Just before
serving add the shrimp fritters.

EASTER SUNDAY

Whatever else is on the table at *comida* on this feast day, there will be *Bacalao a la Vizcaina*, Salt Cod, Basque-style. It is the day when the cooking traditions of Mexico and Spain meet. There is a large Basque colony in Mexico and Basques have contributed a great deal to the country right up to the Presidency. The dish has evolved in Mexico and there are many versions slightly different from each other and from the original. The original itself owes much to Mexico as it depends on Mexican peppers.

Bacalao a la Vizcaina
(SALT COD, BASQUE-STYLE)

serves 4
450g/1lb dried salt cod
2 medium onions, finely chopped
3tablespoons olive oil
3 large garlic cloves
1 slice firm white bread, toasted and chopped
1 sweet red pepper, seeded and chopped
900g/2lbs tomatoes, peeled, seeded and finely
  chopped
5ml/1teaspoon sweet paprika
40ml/2tablespoons parsley, chopped
450g/1lb potatoes, cooked and sliced
125ml/4fl oz dry sherry
salt, freshly ground black pepper

for the garnish:
green olives, triangles of fried bread and canned
  pimiento morrón

1 Soak the cod in cold water overnight. Drain the fish and rinse it in fresh water. Put it into a saucepan with cold water to cover and one of the chopped onions. Bring to a simmer and cook over very low heat for 20 minutes or until the fish is tender. When it is cool enough to handle remove any skin and bones and cut it into 3.5cm/1½in pieces.

2 In a frying-pan heat the oil and fry the garlic over low heat until brown. Remove and discard. Add the remaining onion to the pan and sauté until it is soft.

3 In a food processor or blender combine the toast, pepper, tomatoes and paprika and reduce to a purée. Add to the frying-pan and cook until the mixture is thick and well blended, about 10 minutes. Add the parsley, potatoes, cod, sherry, a little of the water in which the cod was cooked, and salt and pepper to taste. Simmer over very low heat just long enough to heat the mixture through, about 5 minutes. Garnish with the olives, fried bread and slices of *pimiento*

Flan
(CREME CARAMEL)

A favourite Spanish dessert, this is equally popular in France and Mexico. It would be appropriate as the ending to any festive meal or any ordinary *comida* for that matter. Though it can be made in a large caramelized mould, it is much more popular to have small individual custard cups for serving.

serves 6
to caramelize the custard cups:
100g/4oz/½cup sugar
40ml/2tablespoons water

1 Have ready 6 custard cups warmed by standing in hot water.
2 In a small saucepan, over moderate heat, combine the sugar and water and cook, stirring constantly, until the sugar melts and turns a rich golden brown. Divide the caramel among the custard cups, pouring it in and turning the moulds so that the caramel covers the bottom and sides. As soon as it stops running turn the cups upside down on a flat surface.

for the custard:
1litre/1¾pints/4cups milk
175g/6oz/¾cup sugar
8 eggs, lightly beaten
1teaspoon vanilla essence
pinch salt

1 Bring the milk to scalding point in a saucepan over moderate heat. Set aside. In a large bowl beat the sugar gradually into the eggs. Add the milk, vanilla and salt. Mix well, and strain into caramelized custard cups.

2 Place the cups in a baking pan filled with hot water that reaches halfway up the cups and bake in a preheated 180°C/350°F/gas4 oven for 1 hour, or until a knife inserted into the custard comes out clean. While cooking do not let the water in the baking pan come to a boil. Lift out the custard cups and let them cool, then refrigerate.

3 To unmould, run a wet knife between the custard and the mould, then place a plate upside down over the cup and invert it quickly.

Margarita
(TEQUILA COCKTAIL)

Though tequila is often drunk in the traditional way with lime juice and salt, this sophisticated drink has become such a favourite that it is welcome at any time and especially when there is a fiesta. It is important to use fresh lime juice; lemon juice is a poor substitute.

serves 1
cut lime
salt
50ml/2fl oz/3tablespoons white tequila
20ml/1tablespoon Cointreau or Triple Sec
20ml/1tablespoon lime juice
3 or 4 ice cubes

Rub the rim of a cocktail glass with the cut lime, then dip the rim in salt. Combine the remaining ingredients in a mixing glass and stir well. Strain into the prepared cocktail glass.

Día de la Independencia

INDEPENDENCE DAY

This is a double festival, first celebrated in Puebla on St Augustine's Day, 28th August 1821. The 15th September is Mexico's Independence Day. *Chiles en Nogada*, regarded as the national dish, was created to honour the patron saint of Augustin de Iturbide, leader of the forces that finally broke Spain's domination of Mexico. The colours are those of the Mexican flag, green, white and red. Walnuts at this time of year have been freshly harvested and are easy to peel. The nuts are soft and milky and delicately flavoured. Pomegranates, whose seeds are the red of the flag, are also in season and the leaves of flat parsley, the green of the flag, are bright and large. The peppers used are the tapering, very dark green, mild *poblanos* with their rich, subtle flavour. When ripe red and dried, they are the mild, equally rich tasting *chiles ancho*, central to Mexican cooking.

Independence celebrations begin the night before to commemorate the moment when Father Hidalgo gave the *Grito*, the cry to overthrow Spain and liberate the country. Paradoxically he was a priest of Spanish origin. The feasting is the following day when *Chiles en Nogada* will be served at *comida*, the main midday meal. *Flan* will almost certainly end the meal and plenty of tequila will be available for aperitifs. Beer, wine, *pulque* (a Mexican beer made from the *ageve* (century plant) and probably more tequila will be served. Increasingly *margaritas* are the favourite way of serving tequila though the traditional way of taking a lick of salt, downing a straight shot of tequila and ending with a suck of a halved lime is still

popular, especially among the gentlemen riders
dressed in *charro* costumes, elaborate cowboy outfits
with huge *sombreros*, who take part in rodeos on
Sundays and holidays. Puelba is famous for its
candied fruits, especially its peaches, and the
traditional paste of sweet potatoes, coloured and
flavoured and formed into a variety of shapes often to
resemble fruit. These are always available for nibbling
on Sundays and Festival days.

Chiles en Nogada
(GREEN PEPPERS IN FRESH WALNUT SAUCE)

Poblano peppers are seldom available outside
Mexico. The best substitute is large, sweet green
peppers. Many cooks like to dip them in beaten egg
and fry them. They are then served warm with the
cold walnut sauce. Some people like a sweetish sauce
flavoured with a little ground cinnamon. I prefer it
slightly salty. When fresh walnuts are not available,
soak ordinary walnuts overnight.

serves 4–6
6 *poblano* peppers, or 6 large sweet green peppers
pomegranate seeds
flat leafed parsley

for the picadillo stuffing:
40ml/2tablespoons olive or vegetable oil
900g/2lb finely chopped, lean, boneless pork
1 large onion, finely chopped
1 garlic clove, crushed
450g/1lb tomatoes, peeled, seeded and chopped
2 small hot green chiles, seeded and chopped
salt, freshly ground black pepper
1 medium pear, peeled, cored and chopped
1 medium peach, peeled, pitted and chopped
40ml/2tablespoons seedless raisins
40ml/2tablespoons blanched, slivered almonds

1 Heat the oil in a large heavy frying-pan and sauté
the pork until it is lightly browned. Add the onion and
garlic and cook until soft. Spoon off any excess fat.
2 Add the tomatoes, chiles and season to taste and
cook, uncovered, over low heat for 15 minutes. Add
the fruit, raisins and almonds and cook over low heat
for 15 minutes longer. Set aside until ready to stuff the
peppers.

to prepare the poblanos:
1 Impale the peppers on a large fork over a gas flame until the skin blackens and blisters.. Put the pepper in a plastic bag, adding the remaining peppers as they are done. Leave for about 30 minutes then rinse off the thin papery skin.
2 Carefully slit the peppers lengthways and remove the stems, seeds and veins taking care not to cut through. Fill the peppers with the *picadillo* stuffing and set them aside. Fasten them with toothpicks. The batter in which they are fried will seal them.

for the sauce:
100g/4oz/1cup walnut meats, soaked, peeled, patted
    dry and ground fine
225g/8oz/1cup cream cheese, softened
225ml/8fl oz/1cup milk or single cream
20ml/1tablespoon sugar (optional)
pinch of ground cinnamon (optional)

1 In a bowl work the walnuts into the cream cheese, then beat in enough milk or cream to make a sauce the consistency of mayonnaise. If using sugar and cinnamon add them to the sauce at this point.
for the batter:
2 large eggs, separated
salt
flour for dusting the peppers
oil for deep frying

1 In a bowl beat the egg yolks. In another bowl beat the whites until they stand in firm peaks. Combine the egg yolks and whites.
2 Dust the peppers with flour then dip into the egg mixture. Fry the peppers in hot oil until they are golden brown all over.
3 Lift them out onto a serving platter and mask with the sauce. Garnish with pomegranate seeds and sprigs of flat parsley.

Churros
(FRITTERS)

Mexico adopted *churros* from Spain making enough of a change in the ingredients to call them its own. They are named after the *churro*, a Spanish sheep with long coarse hair. They are sold at fairs from small portable cooking stalls called *churrerias* where they go straight from the deep-fryer to the customer. Welcome at any time, they are always found in the market at holiday times and no fiesta would be complete without them. In Mexico a cut up lime is added to the cooking oil giving the *churros* a subtly different flavour.

makes about a dozen
oil for deep frying
1 lime, quartered
2.5ml/½teaspoon salt
20ml/1tablespoon granulated sugar
175g/6oz/1½cups plain flour
2 eggs
caster or confectioner's sugar for dipping

1 Heat the oil in a deep-fryer and add the lime pieces.
2 In a large saucepan combine 225ml/8fl oz/1cup of water with the salt and sugar and bring to a boil. Add the flour, all at once, and beat with a wooden spoon until smooth.
3 Off the heat add the eggs, one at a time and beat until the mixture is satiny. Spoon the mixture into a piping bag fitted with a fluted 1cm/½in nozzle. As soon as the oil reaches 190°C/375°F on a frying thermometer, lift out and discard the lime pieces.
4 Pipe the dough into the oil allowing about 15cm/6in for each *churro* and fry until golden, 3–4 minutes. Drain on paper towels and roll in caster sugar. Eat them warm.

El Platillo Nacional

THE FESTIVAL NATIONAL DISH

Mole Poblano de Guajolote, the great festive dish of Mexico, appropriate for any grand or happy occasion to be served at engagement parties, weddings, christenings, birthdays, anniversaries or family gatherings for Sunday *comida* (lunch). It dates back before the conquest of the country by Spain, and reflects Mexican cuisine, based on sauces. In Nahuatl, the native language, the *mollis* (changed to *moles*, pronounced Molays in Spanish) are innumerable. Puebla de los Angeles, capital of the State of Puebla, south of Mexico City, gives its name to the national dish and the legends surrounding its origin.

When Emperor Moctezuma entertained the Spanish conqueror Hernán Cortés, turkey *mole* was served. In early colonial times legend has it that the dish was invented by Sor Andrea of the Convent of Santa Rosa to honour the visiting Archbishop for having a convent built for her Order. She combined the foods of Old and New Worlds and this makes some sense but the story of Fray Pascual strains credulity. Fray Pascual was in charge of his convent's kitchens when the visiting Viceroy, Don Juan de Palafox y Mendoza, came to dine. Tidying up the kitchen he made a pile of spices and a random wind blew them into the *cazuelas*, earthenware pots, of simmering turkey and changed them into *mole*. The probable truth is that Sor Andrea saved the dish from oblivion by listening to the Aztec girls who had joined the convent.

Chocolate, a royal food, was forbidden to women and all but the higher ranks of the military, clergy and merchants. The girls from the Aztec aristocracy would have known of the dish and would have passed on the recipe. Sor Andrea doubtless added her own

42

refinements, cinnamon and cloves for native allspice for example. She has earned the gratitude of all lovers of good food.

Mole Poblano de Guajolote
(TURKEY IN CHILES AND BITTER CHOCOLATE SAUCE)

serves 8–10
6 *ancho* chiles
4 *pasilla* chiles
4 *mulato* chiles (specialist importers stock these dried chiles)
2.7–3.6kg/6–8lb turkey, cut into serving pieces
salt
75ml/4tablespoons lard
2 medium onions, finely chopped
3 garlic cloves, chopped
100g/4oz blanched almonds, ground
65g/2½oz/½cup seedless raisins
2.5ml/½teaspoon ground cloves
2.5ml/½teaspoon ground cinnamon
2.5ml/½teaspoon ground coriander seeds
1ml/¼teaspoon anise
75ml/4tablespoons sesame seeds
20ml/1tablespoon chopped fresh coriander leaves
1 *tortilla* or slice of white bread, toasted and cut up
450g/1lb tomatoes, peeled, seeded and chopped
40g/1½oz bitter chocolate, broken into bits

1 Break off the stems of the chiles and shake out the seeds. Rinse them in cold water and tear them into pieces. Put them into a bowl with warm water barely to cover and leave to soak for about 1 hour. Set aside until ready to cook.

2 Put the turkey pieces into a large casserole and add enough salted water to cover. Simmer, over low heat, until the turkey is tender, about 1 hour. Drain, reserving the stock. Dry the turkey pieces with paper towels.

3 Heat the lard in a large frying-pan and sauté the turkey pieces, a few at a time, until they are lightly browned. Transfer to a large, heavy casserole, reserving the lard.

4 Combine the onions, garlic, almonds, raisins, cloves, cinnamon, coriander seeds, anise, half the sesame seeds, fresh coriander, *tortilla* or toast, prepared chiles (drained) and the tomatoes in a food processor or blender and reduce to a coarse purée.

5 Heat the lard remaining in the frying-pan, adding if necessary enough to make up the quantity to about 60ml/3tablespoons. Add the purée and cook, stirring constantly with a wooden spoon, for about 5 minutes. Gradually pour in 1litre/16fl oz/2cups of the reserved turkey stock, add the chocolate, season to taste with salt and cook, stirring, until the chocolate has melted and the sauce is smooth and quite thick.

6 Pour the sauce over the turkey and cook, covered, on very low heat for about 30 minutes for the turkey to absorb the flavours. Arrange on a large, heated platter, sprinkle with the remaining sesame seeds and serve with hot *tortillas*, *frijoles* (beans), *guacamole* and plain white rice.

The common bean, is always served, in its dried not fresh form, after the main course at *comida*. I use the recipe given to me by my husband's grandmother, Doña Carmelita Sarabia de Tinoco. Pinto beans were her favourite and would be served even after a main course as hearty as *Mole Poblano*.

Frijoles
(BEANS)

serves 6–8
450g/1lb pinto or red kidney beans
2 medium onions, finely chopped
2 garlic cloves, chopped
1 small hot green chile, seeded and chopped
1 bay leaf
40ml/2tablespoons vegetable oil
1x125g/4oz tomato, peeled and chopped
salt

1 Rinse the beans and put them into a large saucepan
with cold water to cover by about 2.5cm/1in. Add one
of the onions, a clove of garlic, the chile and the bay
leaf. Cover, bring to a simmer and cook over low
heat, adding hot water as needed. As soon as the
beans begin to wrinkle, about 20 minutes, add
1 tablespoon of the oil and continue to cook until the
beans are tender, about 1½ to 2 hours according to
how fresh the beans are.
2 While the beans are cooking heat the rest of the oil
in a frying-pan and sauté the remaining onion and
clove of garlic until soft. Add the tomato and cook
for 3–4 minutes longer.
3 When the beans are soft scoop out half a teacupful
of the beans and add them to the pan bit by bit
mashing them into the onion-tomato mixture, over
low heat, to form a fairly heavy paste. Stir this into the
beans, season with salt and cook over low heat to
thicken the bean liquid and blend the flavours. The
finished beans should be slightly soupy. Serve in
small bowls after the main course and eat with a
spoon.

Frijoles Refritos
(REFRIED BEANS)

Used in many Mexican dishes, you cook the beans in the same way but instead of a small frying-pan to sauté the onion mixture, use a large one and gradually mash all the beans and their liquid to a paste adding 1 tablespoon of lard or vegetable oil from time to time until the beans form a heavy creamy paste. They may be used as a spread or formed into a roll, sprinkled with grated cheese and stuck with triangles of crisply fried *tortillas*, when they are called *tostaditas*. Serve as a side dish.

Guacamole
(AVOCADO SAUCE/SALAD)

One of the oldest of the Aztec dishes, *guacamole* is essential whether the meal it accompanies is festive or everyday. The tall, beautiful avocado tree, *Persea americana*, was first cultivated in Mexico about 7,000BC. Originally the dish was just plain mashed avocado, then tomato and onion were added with hot chiles and, after the Conquest, fresh coriander leaves from that herb which the Spanish had introduced. As the avocado flesh discolours very quickly, *guacamole* should be made at the last minute. The addition of oil and vinegar to prevent discoloration is a mistake as it robs the avocado of its true, exquisite flavour. Piled into a fresh, hot corn *tortilla*, it is an ideal accompaniment to *Mole Poblano*.

serves 8–10
2 large ripe avocados
1x125g/4oz tomato, peeled, seeded and chopped
½ small white onion, finely chopped
1 small fresh hot green chiles, seeded and finely chopped
25g/1oz/½cup coriander leaves chopped
salt

1 Peel and mash the avocados preferably with a fork as the avocados should retain some texture. Fold in the rest of the ingredients and season to taste.

Día de los Muertos

ALL SOULS DAY

On 2nd November, All Souls Day, it is traditional in Mexico to visit the graves of loved ones as a mark of both affection and respect. People take huge bunches of *zempazuchitl*, bright orange marigolds, and a special round coffee cake, *Pan de Muerto* (Bread of the Dead) which is decorated with a cross made of pieces of baked dough in the form of alternating tear-drops and bones with a knob in the centre. Pink sugar crystals decorate the cake. This is not a sad day. It is a picnic in which the dead participate symbolically. Candy skulls are sold inscribed with the names of the picnickers. It is a little disconcerting for those encountering the custom for the first time as one is supposed to nibble away cheerfully at this reminder of the inevitable future. Despite the awful warning that the candy skull conveys everything is lively and brilliant from the blue sky and yellow sun to the orange marigolds to the bright skirts, shirts and *rebozos* (shawls) worn by the members of family parties lovingly tending graves in the family plot. This is no day for mourning, it is a fiesta.

Some of the All Souls celebrations are extremely elaborate suggesting rites belonging to the pre-Christian faith of the region. In Janitzio, the small island in Lake Patzcuaro, Michoacan preparations begin two days before, when the men of the village go duck-hunting, using the traditional harpoon instead of guns. The duck meat is cooked with a chile sauce and used to stuff the *tamales* made by the women of the village. On All Souls Eve, the women take the *tamales* and huge bunches of marigolds and a candle for each family member who has died. With their older children, they keep an all-night vigil at the graves, while the men keep vigil at home. The following day the family has a feast of *tamales* served with *atole*, coffee, *pulque*, beer, tequila and *Pan de Muerto*. It is believed that the dead have already feasted during the night of vigil in a mystical way.

Pan de Muerto
(BREAD OF THE DEAD)

serves about 12
40ml/2tablespoons anise water
20ml/1tablespoon active dry yeast
125ml/4fl oz/½cup lukewarm water
450g/1lb/4cups sifted plain flour
5ml/1tablespoon salt
125g/4oz/½cup sugar
225g/8oz/1cup butter, melted
6 large eggs, lightly beaten
20ml/1tablespoon orange blossom water
grated rind of 1 orange

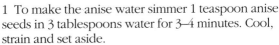

1 To make the anise water simmer 1 teaspoon anise
seeds in 3 tablespoons water for 3–4 minutes. Cool,
strain and set aside.
2 In a bowl proof the yeast with the water for
15 minutes or until foamy. Add enough flour to make
a light dough. Turn it onto a lightly floured board and
knead briefly. Shape the dough into a ball and place
in a warm, draft-free place, covered, to double in
bulk, about 1 hour.
3 Sift the remaining flour with the salt and sugar into
a large bowl. Stir in the melted butter, eggs, orange
blossom water, anise water and the grated orange
rind, mixing thoroughly. Turn out onto a lightly
floured board until smooth. Add the dough and
knead the two together until satiny. Form into a ball
and place, covered, in a warm, draft-free place to rise
until doubled in bulk, about 1½ hours. Shape into
2 round loaves, setting aside dough for decoration.
4 Place the loaves on a greased baking sheet and
decorate with a cross made of pieces of dough
alternately shaped like bones and teardrops. Cover
the loaves and stand in a warm place until again
doubled in bulk.

5 Bake the loaves in a preheated 190°C/375°F/gas5 oven for about 30 minutes or until done. When the bread is cool frost it and sprinkle with coloured sugar crystals. To make the frosting add sifted icing sugar to 50ml/2fl oz/¼cup boiling water or milk until of spreading consistency.

Calabaza Enmielada
(PUMPKIN IN BROWN SUGAR SAUCE)

This is a year-round dish and though it is a dessert is often served for breakfast or at *merienda*, the light supper sometimes preferred as a meal to end the day after the robust *comida*. But its bright orange colour makes it a favourite for All Souls Day. There are many versions of a pumpkin dessert; this is my favourite.

serves 6
1 pumpkin, about 1.4kg/3lb, preferably a thin-
    skinned variety, seeds and strings removed
450g/1lb/2cups dark brown sugar

1 Wipe the pumpkin over with a damp cloth and cut it into wedges. Choose a heavy saucepan or casserole into which the pumpkin can be fitted comfortably, skin side down. Take 350g/12oz/1½cups of the sugar and sprinkle it over the pumpkin wedges, dividing it evenly. Pour about 125ml/4fl oz/½cup water into the pan, cover and cook over very low heat, adding a little more water if necessary, until the pumpkin is tender, about 40 minutes.
2 In a small saucepan combine the rest of the sugar with 50ml/2fl oz/¼cup water and simmer until it is thickened. Serve separately as a sauce. Serve with a glass of milk or you can pour the milk over the pumpkin instead of the sugar syrup.

Virgin de Guadelupe

FEAST DAY OF THE VIRGIN OF GUADALUPE

People from all over Mexico visit the shrine of the Virgin and attend services in the Basilica on 12th December. The shrine, at the foot of Tepeyac hill in the town of La Villa de Guadalupe, is only 3 miles away from Mexico City's cathedral.

Before the Conquest the hill was the site of the shrine of the Aztec goddess of Earth and Corn, Tonantzin, virgin and mother. The first Catholic archbishop of Mexico had it and other Aztec shrines destroyed. On 9th December, 1531, a convert on his way to church had a vision of the Virgin, who told him she wanted a church built on top of the previous shrine. Poor Juan Diego found it hard to convince his bishop who sent him back to find proof. On 12th December, the last time Diego saw her, she sent him to collect pink roses which he found growing among the cacti. He gathered them up in his cloak on which appeared the image of the Virgin. This convinced the bishop and the shrine and Basilica were built. All round the church are stalls selling a great variety of Mexican *antojitos* (snacks), *tacos*, *tamales,* and different *atoles*. A traditional and favourite nibble are *gorditas de la villa*. These fat little maize cakes are made from cooked, ground hominy corn but *masa harina* (flour for *tortillas*) can be used. Economy-minded home cooks are said to wet stale *tortillas* and grind them up into a dough to make *gorditas* but I have never come across them and don't want to.

Gorditas de la Villa
(LITTLE FAT MAIZE CAKES)

makes about 30
450g/1lb *masa harina* (*tortilla* flour)
5ml/1teaspoon baking powder
225g/8oz caster or confectioner's sugar
225g/8oz lard or butter
6 egg yolks, lightly beaten

1 In a bowl, sift together the *tortilla* flour, baking powder and sugar. Rub in the lard or butter with the fingertips to make a coarse crumble. Stir in the egg yolks, adding a little water if necessary, to make a soft dough. Shape into little fat cakes. Traditionally the dough is pinched out to form small points round the edges. Bake on a preheated griddle for 2–3 minutes on each side, turning once. Wrap 3–4 in coloured tissue paper.

Noche de Rábanos

RADISH NIGHT

In Oaxaca, a state where the pre-Colombian past is very present, there is a curious festival on Christmas Eve called *Noche de Rábanos*. Large radishes are in season and they are carved into fancy shapes and used to decorate the market stalls and restaurants around the Plaza of Oaxaca City. The state is famous for its black and beautiful green pottery and all year long the potters save up imperfect plates and dishes. On Radish Night *buñuelos* are served on the pottery and when the revellers finish eating they smash the flawed plates. By midnight the square is a sea of broken crockery. The festive food is, of course, the *buñuelo*.

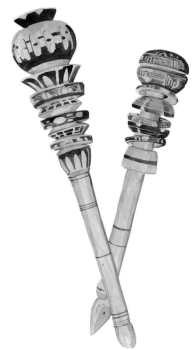

Ponche de Leche, Yemas y Cognac
(CHRISTMAS EGGNOG)

A light eggnog made with milk instead of the more usual cream, it is rich and generously alcoholic without being cloying. It is a popular drink for Christmas to serve at any time with sweet cakes or cookies.

makes 4.5litres/8pints
15 egg yolks
450g/1lb caster or confectioner's sugar
2litres/3½pints milk
20ml/1tablespoon grated orange peel
1 bottle Cognac or other brandy
ground cinnamon

1 Beat the egg yolks with the sugar in a large bowl until light and lemon-coloured. Whisk in the milk. Pour the mixture into the top of a double boiler set over hot water and cook, stirring, on very low heat until the mixture is thick enough to coat the spoon. Remove from the heat and stir in the grated orange peel. Whisk in the brandy and serve warm in 125ml/4oz punch cups, topped with a little cinnamon.

Las Fiestas de Navidad

CHRISTMAS

After the *Posadas*, re-enacting the Holy Family's search for room at an Inn, Mexico celebrates with Midnight Mass followed by a veritable feast. Traditionally the meal begins with a rich chicken consommé enlivened with sherry, followed by a dried salt cod dish. The main course is stuffed roast turkey or turkey in *mole* sauce and *Ensalada de Nochebuena.*

The meal reflects the colonial influences in Mexican cooking with New and Old World foods combining, the turkey a New World bird domesticated by the Aztecs and salt codfish very much a Spanish favourite, avocados and chiles indigenous foods, apples, almonds and raisins introduced. There are cakes, biscuits, nuts, fruits both fresh and dried, *buñuelos* and *gaznates* and sweetmeats to round out the feast. And to drink there is beer, wine, sparkling cider, fruit drinks and especially tequila. Children are not given their presents until January 6th, the day when the Three Kings came with their gifts for the infant Jesus.

It is the most colourful of all the fiestas, from the midnight church ablaze with light to the family table loaded with food and decorated with the scarlet brilliance of the Christmas flower, poinsettia.

Sopa Seca Para Navidad
('DRY' SOUP FOR CHRISTMAS)

The curiously named dry soup is a rice, pasta or
tortilla dish that follows the *sopa aguada* (wet soup).
Rice and pasta were both unknown to the Aztecs who
invented the term *sopa seca* to describe the unknown
dishes. This one is special for the festive Christmas
Eve dinner.

serves 4–6
225g/8oz thin *macaroni*, or use *penne, fusilli* or other
   pasta
20ml/1tablespoon salt
100g/4oz/1cup mild Cheddar cheese, grated
40ml/2tablespoons chopped parsley
butter for greasing baking dish and topping sauce

for the bechamel:
40ml/2tablespoons butter
40ml/2tablespoons flour
225ml/8fl oz/1cup milk
salt, freshly ground white pepper

for the tomato sauce:
20ml/1tablespoon olive or vegetable oil
1 small onion, finely chopped
1 garlic clove, chopped
1 sweet red pepper, peeled, seeded and chopped
450g/1lb tomatoes, peeled and chopped
salt, freshly ground black pepper
1ml/¼teaspoon sugar
10ml/2teaspoons tomato purée
50ml/2fl oz/¼cup water

1 Bring a large saucepan of salted water to a brisk boil. Add the pasta, stir and boil, uncovered, until the pasta is tender, about 10 minutes. Drain and set aside.

2 To make the béchamel, heat the butter in a saucepan and stir in the flour with a wooden spoon. Cook over low heat, stirring, without letting the mixture colour, for 2 minutes. Remove from the heat and gradually add the milk stirring to mix, until the sauce is smooth. Season with salt and pepper, return to the heat and cook, stirring, over low heat for 5 minutes. Set aside.

3 Make the tomato sauce by heating the oil in a saucepan and sauté the onion, garlic and sweet red pepper until the vegetables are soft. Add the tomatoes, salt, pepper, sugar and tomato purée, and simmer over low heat. If the mixture is at all dry, add a little water. Continue to simmer, uncovered, until the sauce is well blended, stirring from time to time for about 15 minutes. Measure the sauce. There should be 225ml/8fl oz/ 1cup. If necessary reduce over brisk heat or add water to make up the quantity. Press the sauce through a sieve set over a bowl, rubbing the solids through.

4 To assemble the dish, butter a 2litre/3½pints/8cup baking dish generously. Make a layer of half the pasta and top with the tomato sauce. Sprinkle with half the grated cheese and top with the rest of the pasta. Finish the dish with the béchamel sauce and the remaining cheese. Dot with butter and bake in a preheated 180°C/350°F/gas4 oven for 20–30 minutes or until the dish is heated through and the top lightly browned. Serve garnished with parsley.

La Nochebuena

CHRISTMAS EVE

After Midnight Mass, instead of the more traditional turkey, this is a popular dish for the Christmas Eve festive dinner.

Pollo en Salsa de Castañas
(CHICKEN IN CHESTNUT SAUCE)

serves 6

1.6kg/3½lb chicken, cut into serving pieces
2 onions, chopped
bouquet garni: sprig of thyme and marjoram and 1 bay leaf tied together with thread
125ml/4fl oz/½cup dry white wine
1litre/1¾pints/4cups chicken stock
salt, freshly ground black pepper
450g/1lb whole peeled chestnuts (canned) or equivalent fresh
450g/1lb tomatoes, peeled and chopped
125ml/4fl oz/½cup double or heavy cream
60ml/2fl oz/4tablespoons medium dry sherry

1 Put the chicken pieces into a heavy casserole with one of the onions, the bouquet garni, dry white wine and enough chicken stock to cover. Season to taste with salt and pepper, cover and simmer over very low heat until the chicken is tender, about 45 minutes. Lift the chicken out to a dish, cover and keep warm. Pour the chicken stock into a bowl and skim off as much fat as possible.

2 In a food processor combine the chestnuts, tomatoes and second onion with 225ml/8fl oz/1cup of the stock and reduce to a purée. Transfer to a casserole and thin to a sauce consistency with as much of the remaining chicken stock as needed. Simmer, covered, over low heat to blend the flavours for 5 minutes.

3 Add the cream, sherry and chicken pieces and cook, over very low heat, for just long enough to heat the chicken through. Serve with plenty of plain rice.

Ensalada de Noche Buena

(CHRISTMAS EVE SALAD)

In the past the salad dressing was simply 100g/4oz/
½cup sugar mixed with 3–4 tablespoons wine
vinegar. Nowadays mayonnaise or oil and vinegar
dressing
(3 parts oil to 1 part vinegar, salt and pepper) are
preferred. *Jícama* is a Mexican root vegetable which
looks rather like a turnip and is eaten raw. The flesh is
crisp and fresh tasting. Tart cooking apples are the
best substitute if *jícamas* are not available.

serves 6–8
3 medium beetroot, cooked, peeled and coarsely
   chopped
3 oranges, peeled and sectioned
2 small *jícamas*, or 2 tart cooking apples, peeled,
   cored and chopped
2 bananas, peeled and sliced
3 slices fresh pineapple, cut into cubes
lettuce leaves
50g/2oz/½cup chopped peanuts
seeds from 1 pomegranate
125ml/4fl oz/½cup mayonnaise or vinaigrette (oil and
   vinegar dressing)
1 stick sugar cane, peeled and chopped (optional)

1 In a bowl mix together the beetroot, orange
segments, *jícamas* or apples, bananas and pineapple
and chill thoroughly.
2 Line a salad bowl with the lettuce leaves and pile
the salad in the centre. Garnish the salad with the
peanuts and pomegranate seeds. Serve the
mayonnaise or vinaigrette separately. If the sugar cane
is available, add it to the salad.